ABILITY

"I can do all things through Christ which strengtheneth me."

–Philippians 4:13
The Holy Bible

Nothing Is Ever As Difficult As It First Appears. *-MIKE MURDOCK*

2

ACHIEVEMENT

"Verily, verily, I say unto you, He that believeth on Me, the works that I do shall he do also; and greater works than these shall he do; because I go unto My Father."

–John 14:12
The Holy Bible

The Quality Of Your Preparation Determines The Quality Of Your Performance. *-MIKE MURDOCK*

3

ADVERSITY

"When thou passest through the waters, I will be with thee; and through the rivers, they shall not overflow thee: when thou walkest through the fire, thou shalt not be burned; neither shall the flame kindle upon thee."

–Isaiah 43:2
The Holy Bible

Warfare Always Surrounds The Birth Of A Miracle.

-MIKE MURDOCK

4

ASSIGNMENT

"Then the word of the Lord came unto me, saying, Before I formed thee in the belly I knew thee; and before thou camest forth out of the womb I sanctified thee, and I ordained thee a prophet unto the nations."

–Jeremiah 1:4-5
The Holy Bible

Your Assignment On Earth Is Simply The Problem God Created You To Solve. *-MIKE MURDOCK*

5

ASSOCIATIONS

"He that walketh with wise men shall be wise: but a companion of fools shall be destroyed."

–Proverbs 13:20
The Holy Bible

Those Who Do Not Increase You Will Inevitably Decrease You.

-MIKE MURDOCK

6

BUSINESS

"Seest thou a man diligent in his business? he shall stand before kings; he shall not stand before mean men."

–Proverbs 22:29
The Holy Bible

Business Is Simply Solving A Problem For Someone For An Agreed Reward. *-MIKE MURDOCK*

7

CHARACTER

"Let integrity and uprightness preserve me; for I wait on Thee."

–Psalm 25:21
The Holy Bible

You Cannot Be What You Are Not, But You Can Become What You Are Not. *-MIKE MURDOCK*

8

CONFRONTATION

"A soft answer turneth away wrath: but grievous words stir up anger."

–Proverbs 15:1
The Holy Bible

Words Are Bridges, Doors, Windows Or Walls.

-MIKE MURDOCK

9

CRITICISM

"For by thy words thou shalt be justified, and by thy words thou shalt be condemned."

–Matthew 12:37
The Holy Bible

Never Spend More Time On A Critic Than You Would Give To A Friend.

-MIKE MURDOCK

10

DEADLINES

"Redeeming the time, because the days are evil."

–Ephesians 5:16
The Holy Bible

What You Finish Is More Important Than What You Begin.

-MIKE MURDOCK

11

DEBT

"The rich ruleth over the poor, and the borrower is servant to the lender."

–Proverbs 22:7
The Holy Bible

Debt Is Birthed By A Spirit That Wants A Harvest It Has Not Yet Earned.

-MIKE MURDOCK

12

DECISION-MAKING

"Trust in the Lord with all thine heart; and lean not unto thine own understanding. In all thy ways acknowledge Him, and He shall direct thy paths."

-Proverbs 3:5-6
The Holy Bible

Champions Make Decisions That Create The Future They Desire, While Losers Make Decisions That Create The Present They Desire. *-MIKE MURDOCK*

13

DELEGATION

"And if ye have not been faithful in that which is another man's, who shall give you that which is your own?"

–Luke 16:12
The Holy Bible

You Can Only Be Promoted By The Person Whose Instruction You Have Followed. *-MIKE MURDOCK*

14

DISCRETION

"Discretion shall preserve thee, understanding shall keep thee."

-Proverbs 2:11
The Holy Bible

Never Discuss Your Problem With Someone Incapable Of Solving It.

-MIKE MURDOCK

15

FAILURES

"Cast thy burden upon the Lord, and He shall sustain thee: He shall never suffer the righteous to be moved."

–Psalm 55:22
The Holy Bible

All Men Fall, The Great Ones Get Back Up. *-MIKE MURDOCK*

16

FAITH

"Therefore I say unto you, What things soever ye desire, when ye pray, believe that ye receive them, and ye shall have them."

-Mark 11:24

The Holy Bible

Faith Comes When The Word Of God Enters You. *-MIKE MURDOCK*

17

FEAR

"Be strong and of a good courage, fear not, nor be afraid of them: for the Lord thy God, He it is that doth go with thee; He will not fail thee, nor forsake thee."

–Deuteronomy 31:6
The Holy Bible

Your Success Is Determined By What You Are Willing To Ignore.

-MIKE MURDOCK

18

FOCUS

"And Jesus said unto him, No man, having put his hand to the plough, and looking back, is fit for the kingdom of God."

–Luke 9:62
The Holy Bible

The Only Reason Men Fail Is Broken Focus. *-MIKE MURDOCK*

19

GOAL-SETTING

"For which of you, intending to build a tower, sitteth not down first, and counteth the cost, whether he have sufficient to finish it?"

-Luke 14:28
The Holy Bible

You Will Never Leave Where You Are, Until You Decide Where You Would Rather Be. *-MIKE MURDOCK*

20

GUIDANCE

"I will instruct thee and teach thee in the way which thou shalt go: I will guide thee with Mine eye."

–Psalm 32:8
The Holy Bible

The Proof Of Humility Is The Willingness To Ask.

-MIKE MURDOCK

21

PASSION

"Whatsoever thy hand findeth to do, do it with thy might; for there is no work, nor device, nor knowledge, nor wisdom, in the grave, whither thou goest."

–Ecclesiastes 9:10
The Holy Bible

You Only Qualify For What You Pursue. *-MIKE MURDOCK*

22

PRAYER

"Confess your faults one to another, and pray one for another, that ye may be healed. The effectual fervent prayer of a righteous man availeth much."

–James 5:16
The Holy Bible

One Hour In The Presence Of God Will Reveal Any Flaw In Your Most Carefully Laid Plans. *-MIKE MURDOCK*

23

PROMOTION

"Wisdom is the principal thing; therefore get wisdom: and with all thy getting get understanding. Exalt her, and she shall promote thee: she shall bring thee to honour, when thou dost embrace her."

–Proverbs 4:7-8

The Holy Bible

You Will Never Be Promoted Until You Become Over-Qualified For Your Present Position. *-MIKE MURDOCK*

24

PROSPERITY

"If they obey and serve Him, they shall spend their days in prosperity, and their years in pleasures."

–Job 36:11
The Holy Bible

Prosperity Is Having Enough Of God's Provision To Complete His Instructions For Your Life.

-MIKE MURDOCK

25

REPUTATION

"A good name is rather to be chosen than great riches, and loving favour rather than silver and gold."

–Proverbs 22:1
The Holy Bible

You Will Only Be Remembered In Life For Two Things: The Problems You Solve Or The Ones You Create.

-MIKE MURDOCK

26

REST

"Come unto Me, all ye that labour and are heavy laden, and I will give you rest."

–Matthew 11:28
The Holy Bible

When Fatigue Walks In Faith Walks Out. *-MIKE MURDOCK*

27

STRESS

"Casting all your care upon Him; for He careth for you."

–1 Peter 5:7
The Holy Bible

Never Complain About What You Permit. *-MIKE MURDOCK*

28

STRUGGLE

"Being confident of this very thing, that He which hath begun a good work in you will perform it until the day of Jesus Christ."

–Philippians 1:6
The Holy Bible

Struggle Is The Proof You Have Not Yet Been Conquered.

-MIKE MURDOCK

29

TEAMWORK

"Two are better than one; because they have a good reward for their labour. For if they fall, the one will lift up his fellow: but woe to him that is alone when he falleth; for he hath not another to help him up."

–Ecclesiastes 4:9-10

The Holy Bible

What You Make Happen For Others, God Will Make Happen For You.

-MIKE MURDOCK

30

TITHING

"Honour the Lord with thy substance, and with the firstfruits of all thine increase: So shall thy barns be filled with plenty, and thy presses shall burst out with new wine."

–Proverbs 3:9-10
The Holy Bible

Tithe Is A Measure Of Your Obedience, An Offering Is A Measure Of Your Generosity.

-MIKE MURDOCK

31

WISDOM

"If any of you lack wisdom, let him ask of God, that giveth to all men liberally, and upbraideth not; and it shall be given him."

–James 1:5
The Holy Bible

The Only Problem You Will Ever Have Is A Wisdom Problem.

-MIKE MURDOCK

DECISION

Will You Accept Jesus As Your Personal Savior Today?

The Bible says, "That if thou shalt confess with thy mouth the Lord Jesus, and shalt believe in thine heart that God hath raised Him from the dead, thou shalt be saved" (Romans 10:9).

Pray this prayer from your heart today! *"Dear Jesus, I believe that You died for me and rose again on the third day. I confess I am a sinner...I need Your love and forgiveness...Come into my heart. Forgive my sins. I receive Your eternal life. Confirm Your love by giving me peace, joy and supernatural love for others. Amen."*

☐ Yes, Mike! I prayed to Jesus today and asked Him to be the King of my life. Please send me my free gift of your book *31 Keys To A New Beginning* to help me with my new life in Christ.

Name ______________________ Birthdate ___/___

Address ______________________

City __________ State ______ Zip __________

Phone (_____) __________ E-Mail __________

Mail to:

The Wisdom Center

4051 Denton Hwy. · Ft. Worth, TX 76117

1-817-759-BOOK · 1-817-759-0300

You Will Love Our Website...! www.WisdomOnline.com

Unless otherwise indicated, all Scripture quotations are taken from the King James Version of the Bible.

31 Scriptures Every Achiever Should Memorize
ISBN 1-56394-227-5/B-183

Editor/Publisher: Deborah Murdock Johnson
Published by The Wisdom Center · 4051 Denton Hwy. · Ft. Worth, TX 76117
1-817-759-BOOK · 1-817-759-0300
You Will Love Our Website...! www.WisdomOnline.com